VINTAGE

AMERICAN-MADE

GLASS CHRISTMAS ORNAMENTS

Jody L. Pritzl

Layout Design by Alex Zezza

DEDICATION

Thanks to the Golden Glow of Christmas Past, the keepers of holiday history and ornament rescuers for saving every precious bulb.

ALSO BY JODY L. PRITZL

Immigrants, Ornaments and Legacies-A Story of American-Made Glass Christmas Ornaments

That Championship Year-The Story of the 1980 Washington High School Raiders of Two Rivers, Wisconsin

Dear Hopeful, Letters From a Friend, Newly Retired

Subscribe to Jody's YouTube channel to see her Christmas ornament videos

Visit booksbyjody.com

TABLE OF CONTENTS

INTRODUCTION
A Christmas ornament has a story.

Who bought it, where and when, a time capsule of tradition and heritage. Tucked away in millions of attics and closets, the vintage ones, bought for a nickel or one dollar for a dozen are being rescued. Once again, they reflect light in their mirror-like finish.

My ornament curiosity began fifty years ago. Each Christmas, I was awed, hanging my grandmother's Shiny Brite ornaments on her artificial tree. I even loved the Uncle Sam and Santa Box that protected the ornaments. Years later, with my own home and Christmas traditions, I remembered the beauty of Grandma Katy's ornaments dating to the 1940s and bought a few Shiny Brites to hang on my tree.

I spent ten years researching and writing a book about the history and companies that were instrumental in developing the 20th-century market for Christmas ornaments. In *Immigrants, Ornaments and Legacies-A Story of American-Made Glass Ornaments*, I wrote about Max Eckardt and Sons, Corning Glass Works, George Franke Sons Company, National Tinsel, B. Wilmsen, and Premier Glass Works.

Readers of the book and YouTube viewers of my ornament videos asked for a reference to help identify their ornaments-manufacturer, decorator, type, and time period. I had been working on this for years but the prompting pushed me to finish the task.

Now for anything wonderful to happen, it must be understood there were two manufacturers of American-made glass Christmas ornaments: Premier Glass Works and Corning Glass Works. All other firms, Max Eckardt's Shiny Brites, George Franke Sons, Coby Glass, Mirostar, and others, were decorators and sellers of Corning Glass bulbs.

With thousands of color and design combinations, this publication represents popular American-made glass ornaments from 1939 through the 1960s. Where I have evidence of a Shiny Brite design or shape debut, I have referenced the approximate year.

Have fun enhancing or starting your vintage ornament collection. Fair warning, treasure hunting, and rescuing bulbs can be habit-forming.

Merry Christmas

-Jody L. Pritzl

PRICE

COLLECTING & PROTECTING VINTAGE ORNAMENTS

Since Premier Glass Works and Corning Glass both manufactured ornaments beginning in 1939, some vintage American ornaments are eighty years old, most existing for a half-century. Fragile, there are fewer available each year. Persevere. By scouring local antique stores, estate sales, and eBay, you can rescue your own beauties.

Dust on ornaments can be swept with a paintbrush; my preference is the fan style. Caps can be cleaned using denatured alcohol or WD-40.

Finding original sets of ornaments is increasingly difficult as bulbs have been swapped between cartons. Many times, an ornament box has been tossed; a disappointment since the packages add a touch of pizazz underneath a Christmas tree. Some collectors focus on a specific color, a time period such as World War II, or a specific design or shape.

Torn cellophane on ornament boxes can be replaced with 4mil Mylar film attached with double-sided specialty adhesive.

My vintage ornament collection began as a hunt for every color of the Shiny Brite bulb Merry Christmas with Holly Spray. Roaming antique stores, I acquired eleven colors of my favorite design and moved on to collecting sufficient Shiny Brites to decorate a six-foot tree. Then I discovered George Franke Sons' decorated bulbs which were also made by Corning.
I'm still buying for the multiple trees I display each Christmas. Throughout the year, for seasonal trees, I hang my solid color ornaments as filler. Red bulbs for Valentine's Day, green for St. Patrick's Day, pink and purple for Easter, making vintage glass ornaments a year-round tradition.

Sometimes, I store the earlier ornaments in their original boxes. Primarily though, my collection is stored in plastic bins to protect the bulbs from extreme hot and cold temperatures. I have grouped the baubles by Shiny Brite, George Franke, or Premiere Glass Works and then by shape or design. Each ornament is wrapped, bagged, and numbered so that after defrocking a tree it can be placed back where it belongs, making it easy to create different themed and color schemed trees.

In 1921 Premier Miniature Bulb Company in Newark, New Jersey was a lighting manufacturer. By the late 1930s, the firm became Premier Glass Works, a maker of Christmas ornaments. Glass was blown in two New Jersey facilities in Irvington and Hoboken where once Lionel manufactured model trains.

Premier ornaments resulted from the work of three men. Walter Gebauer, a talented tool maker for fifteen years worked with his brother Adam Gebauer who was a glass chemist by trade. Intertwined and friends with the Gebauer brothers was Angelo Paione an inventor and expert in machine technology.

Equipment to blow laboratory glass and light bulbs was modified to create Christmas ornaments and in 1939, Premier Glass Works began selling bulbs to customers like Sears Roebuck Company.

The initial Premier ornament types were ovals, bells, clusters, reflectors, and lanterns competing with Corning Glass Works that initially blew only round bulbs. Premier existed until about 1955 when the firm was acquired by the Eckardts who required more capacity as Shiny Brite sales soared. The Gebauer brothers retired and Angelo Paione founded his own ornament company, Paragon Glass Works.

Only Premier Glass Works manufactured a 4" Oblong, possibly as early as 1935 certainly by 1939. The bulb was hand striped and the tinsel inserted manually. Various colors exist of the early oblong and a 3" version is possible to be acquired.

EARLY YEARS

Round

Early Reflector-Red, blue, and white stripes were added later.

Premier caps were modified over time. There are plain slot caps, Premier brand, and Premier Made in USA.

Star Reflector

The first Premier bells were 1 ½" to 1 ¾"

Ribbed Ball

Cluster

Premier entered the market with a limited number of styles. Premier silvered their bulbs on the exterior, a distinctive look.

WAR YEAR TRANSPARENTS

With the United States entry into World War II, ingredients to blend silvering solutions became scarce. Transparents, with metal caps, date to around 1942-1943 or 1946-Forward.

Carriage Lantern

Striped Bell

Railroad Lantern

Striped Round

Early Striped Bell

Teardrop

CARDBOARD CAPS

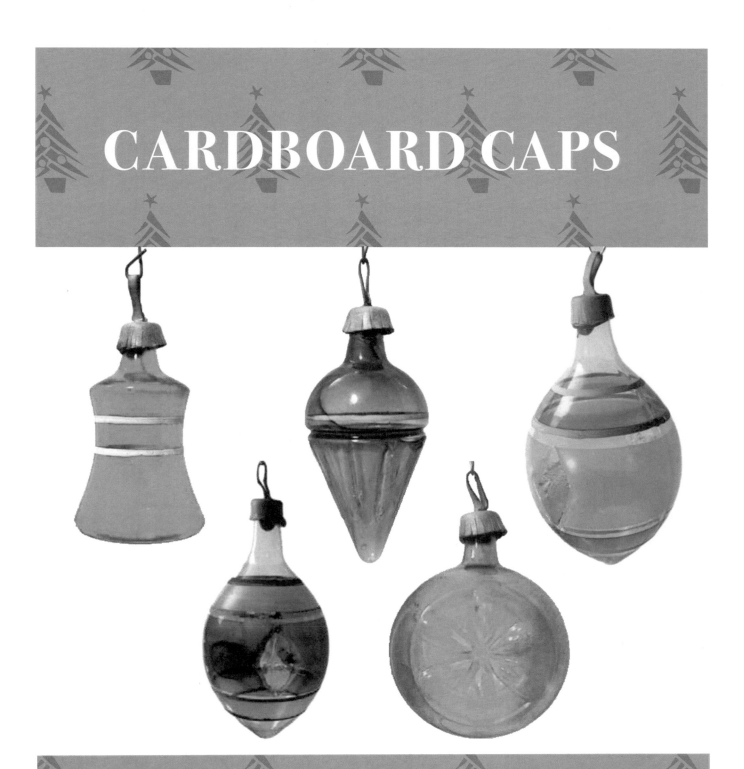

After metal was diverted for the war effort, Premier ornaments were sold with cardboard caps in the years of 1944 and 1945.

Teardrop Reflector

Star Reflector

Twist

Twist

Center Star

Spinning Top

Railwood Lantern

Bell

POST WAR

1946-1955

After World War II, and the return of chemicals, Premier resumed selling silvered and painted ornaments.

Modern Premiers used a plain-rounded edge metal cap

Star Reflector

Belly Spear Point

Spear Point

Some Premier assortments were sold by color scheme, red or blue, identified on side panels The original Premier boxes were printed with red, blue and green ink.

MANUFACTURER

CORNING GLASS WORKS

From the 1880s to the 1930s, most ornaments sold in the United States were imported from Europe. Families, many in German homes, blew hot glass into wooden molds. After the glass cooled, a homemade silvering solution was added and the fragile bulbs were hand-painted before shipment to American retailers. A series of tariffs impacted global trade and before the United States entered World War II, a domestic source of Christmas ornaments became critical.

Working in secret, Corning Glass Works in Wellsboro, Pennsylvania converted a light bulb machine in 1939 to blow glass Christmas ornaments.

Molten glass became a round bulb after compressed air forced expansion. Bulbs cooled for twenty minutes by traveling on a forty-foot belt. Workers, typically female, inspected bulbs for flaws, and then placed the fragile spheres on racks for silvering. After the dyeing process, a bulb's neck was cut and caps with spring loops were inserted by hand. Bulbs were packed in trays for bulk shipment to decorating firms that added unique paint schemes and designs. During the peak years of the 1950s, the Corning plant in Wellsboro produced over 100 million bulbs.

Original colors were blue, red, green, silver and gold in sizes of 1 ¾" or 2 ½"

In December of 1939, Corning Glass Works sold only one million mass produced American made bulbs to decorating firms, and essentially missed the majority of the Christmas retail season. In 1940 Corning blew forty million bulbs. The plain spheres were sent to K and W Glass Works the Shiny Brite decorating partner and George Franke Sons Company.

Corning blown bulbs are a seamless hollow body.

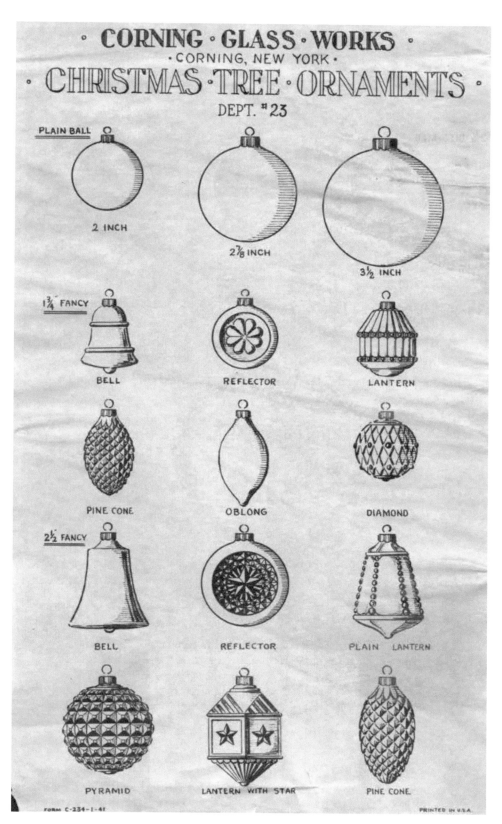

(Courtesy of the Rakow Research Library, Corning, New York)

17

Beaded Lantern-1941

Tic Tac Toe Lantern-1941

Star Lantern-1941

Lantern-1939
Gold and Red also common colors

Lanterns, sometimes considered a symbol of Christ's birth, were blown in several Corning styles

Stout Bells

Long Bell   Grapes

Early Corning Glass bulbs were sold in a single color with shapes that mimicked imported European designs.

DECORATOR
MAX ECKARDT & SONS
SHINY BRITES

Max Eckardt, a German immigrant arrived in the United States in 1909. After pedaling toys, he changed careers to the more lucrative importing trade. To learn the logistics, Max worked for a fellow German, Jewish merchant August Strauss. The two men became partners in Strauss-Eckardt, selling notions, fancy goods, and toys, adding to their product line German Christmas ornaments sold to Woolworth's stores.

When German tariffs were lowered, the business grew, creating healthy profits for Max exporting Christmas ornaments from his factory in Germany. Sentiment changed in the 1920s and 1930s when a 60% tariff was applied to German toys and Christmas ornaments.

By 1938 a boycott was called on U.S. firms sourcing goods from Germany including Strauss-Eckardt. Max, his ornament business in jeopardy, partnered with a friend and fellow German immigrant, Otto Kohler to decorate Corning mass produced bulbs. Shiny Brites expanded to four New Jersey factories with the acquisitions of K & W Glass Works and Premier Glass Works. In the 1950s, Shiny Brites had 50 percent market share of American-made glass Christmas ornaments. Max, leveraged the Good House Keeping seal of approval and mass merchandising to create an iconic American brand.

Max, the gregarious-optimistic business leader, (right) sold his Shiny Brite firm to Thor Manufacturing in 1955. Son Harold stayed with the firm until a series of sales and mergers involving Philips Electronics, Eckmar, and Poloron. (Photo courtesy of the Corning Incorporated Department of Archives and Records Management, Corning, New York)

PRE WAR STRIPES

Otto Kohler, a glass blower from Lauscha, Germany with partner Fred Walter formed K & W Glass Works. For a short time, Otto employed a few men to blow ornaments but K & W would be forever linked with Max Eckardt's Shiny Brites. In 1940 Otto designed a method to decorate glass bulbs and was awarded a patent in 1943. Corning shipped silvered and dyed bulbs to Otto in New Jersey where they were painted using horizontal jigs, brushes, and screens. Adding pizazz to plain round bulbs, the original stripe colors were blue, white, and yellow.

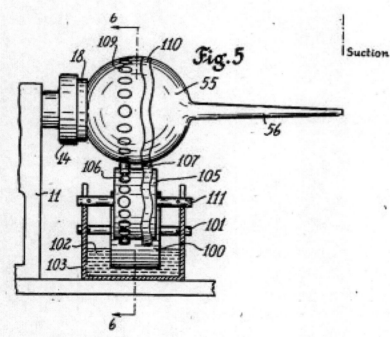

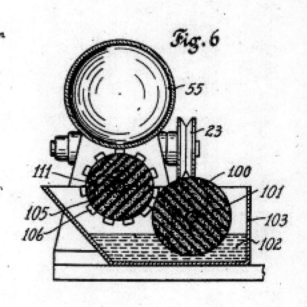

INVENTOR
Otto Kohler

22

Manufactured by the Scovill Manufacturing Company, the Corning cap used from 1939-1943 and 1946-Forward was scalloped but stamped Made in US of A.

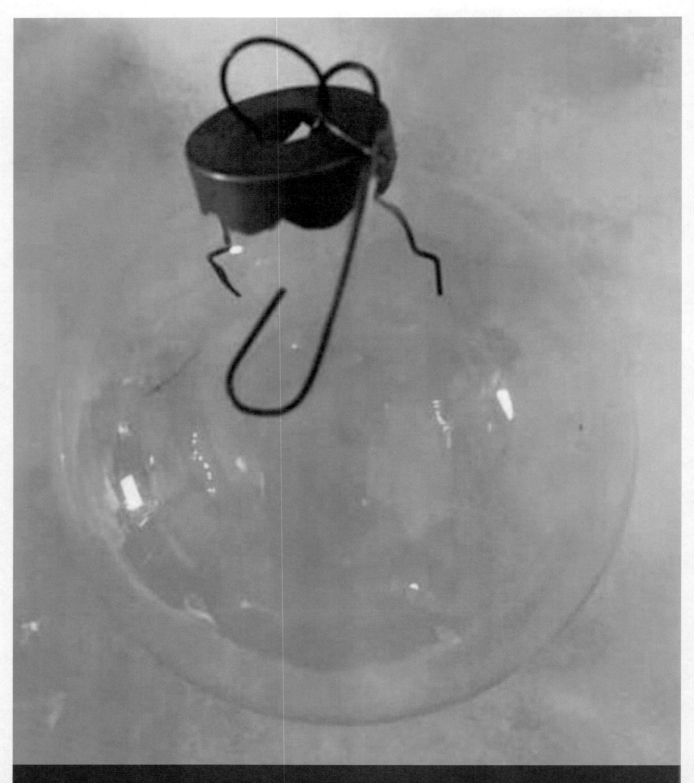

In 1942 scarcity of silver nitrate began and by 1943 transparent bulbs became the defacto standard. Some were painted at K & W Glass Works in New Jersey and sold as Shiny Brites.

TINSEL ORNAMENTS

**Tinsel styles include Tree,
Long Branch, and Multi-Colored.**

Tinsel was invented in Germany and inserted into Christmas ornaments. To add sparkle to transparents, especially during 1940-1942, tinsel was inserted into rounds, oblongs, and bells at the K and W Glass factories and sold as Shiny Brites.

SPECIALTY OBLONGS, ROUNDS, BELL

Handpainted

CARDBOARD CAPS

By 1944 metal caps were no longer available. After just five years of American made bulbs, necessity created the solution of cardboard caps to hang Christmas ornaments during the war years.

There were at least four styles of cardboard caps: Diamond, Loop, Circle, and a combination utilizing a cardboard cap with metal spring loop.

Typically women were employed in decorating factories some as artists. Talented, they painted scroll works, flower petals, and a style called Frosted Leaf or Frosted Snowcap.

Purple and Rose were introduced as
colors in 1944

Diamond Cardboard Cap   Blue Round with Tinsel

An unusual transparent that utilizes a hybrid cardboard and metal cap. The stripes might have been applied by machine but the scroll design was hand-painted.

Shiny Brite introduced opaque paint in 1943. The bulb colors were red, blue, green, and white in styles of round, oval, and bell. When metal caps returned, opaques continued to be sold. An opaque could have a metal cap or a cardboard cap. Over the decades, ornament caps have been switched and swapped.

STRIPES

Originally called a three-stripe technically there are four painted stripes.

In 1946 metal caps returned and the first all striped round assortment was introduced. Four stripe rounds were popular in the 1950s and eventually, the number of stripes increased to six.

Common Shiny Brite caps used after 1947 were branded with a corrugated edge. Since Shiny Brite and George Franke both sourced bulbs from Corning Glass the caps are interchangeable but not properly sized for a Premier Glass ornament.

The blue-white-yellow
stripe configuration

To enliven a plain silver round, stripes were added and scroll work painted on the band.

REFLECTORS

Building on the popularity of European reflectors, American manufacturers debuted a single indent in the 1940s. The shape was refreshed in 1950 with the introduction of double reflectors and eventually, triple reflectors were blown by Corning and decorated by Shiny Brites. Consumers paid on average 30% more for a reflector than a plain round.

Common reflectors are Single, Double, Triple, Star, Sunburst, Colored Center, and Multicolored

Frosted Star   High Spear Point   Oval Star

Bumpy   Star   Striped Oval

Frosted Teardrop   Oval Center    Star Reflector    Sunburst

FANCIES

Technically, any ornament that is not round could be called a Fancy.

Christmas Tree-1952

Frosted Teardrop

Chinese Lantern

Mushroom with Frosted Rim

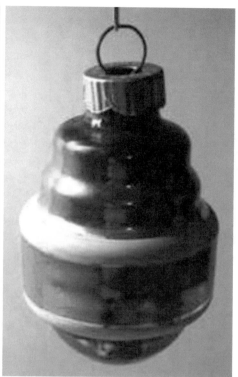

Short Spinning Top-1954   Bee Hive-1959

Crystal Spinning Top   Diamond Cluster or Quilted-1952

Spinning Top

High Drop

Ribbed Oval

Barrel

At times named a barrel more
commonly called Lantern-1954

Carriage Lantern with Crystal Rims

Grape Cluster-1956   Grape Cluster note the lack of stem

Twist-1956

Shiny Brite and Premier Glass Twists are identical with speculation that Premier might have been the manufacturer, not Corning Glass Works. There is a seam on all twists but many instances of twists with Shiny Brite caps but fewer with a Premier cap.

Carriage Lamp

Walnut

Acorn-1956

Wine Keg

Party Lantern

Bells

Since the 1880s in Germany, bells have been a popular Christmas ornament style. Said to have rung for one hour the night of the Christ child's birth, bells were also thought to ward off evil. In the 1940s and 1950s American-made bells were introduced invoking nostalgia for choirs and schoolhouses.

Stout Bell

Clap Bell-1954

Striped Bell

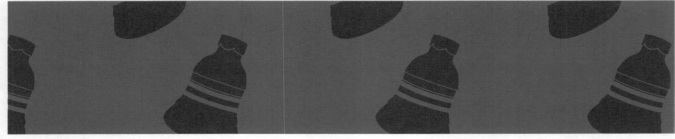

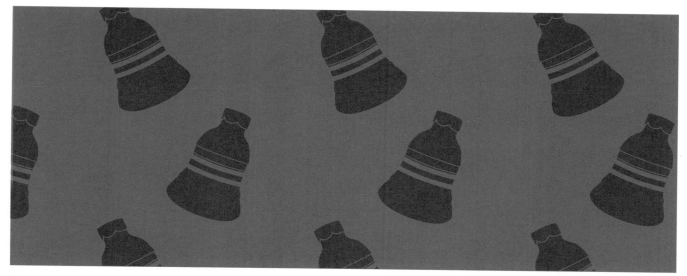

High Bell   Crystal Bell   Frosted Snowcap Bell

SCENIC DESIGNS

To encourage new purchases, designs were freshened annually with the peak years 1947 to 1957.

Star of Bethleham-1949

Skiing Snowman-1950

Stage coach-1954

Deer Scene-1952 uses tree design
from Christmas Village-1949

White Christmas-1955

Santa with Sleigh-1948

Merry Christmas with Holly
Spray- 1949

Merry Christmas with Leaves
Spray- 1948

Merry Christmas with Poinsettia
Spray- 1951

Christmas Joy- 1951

Christmas Greetings- 1955

Night Before Christmas

Merry Christmas
Happy New Year

Christmas Village-1949

Village Carolers   Peace on Earth   Ringing Bells-1948

Holly Spray and Candle-1948   Toy Scene-1950   Stockings

Silent Night With Church-1958

Silent Night Animated Tune-1949

Jingle Bells Animated Tune-1951

Little Bo Peep-1953

Jack and Jill-1953

Humpty Dumpty-1952

A single nursery rhyme was typically included with eleven different ornaments in an assortment.

Stars-1949   Solar System-1958   Candy Colored 1968

SCROLL WORKS

1960's Assortment

UNUSUALS

Scenic designs were added to many shapes. This teardrop uses the Holly Spray with Candle graphic.

A Shiny Brite design called Hammer began in 1949. Gold, silver, blue, pink, and green were used to reintroduce bells, ovals, and rounds

During the war, the technology of adding dots to bells was perfected in 1944.
Invoking a homemade feel, the style was not very popular and costly to manufacture.

K and W Glass Works, owned by Otto Kohler, decorated Corning Glass bulbs for Max Eckardt in North Bergen, New Jersey and West New York, New Jersey. Shiny Brites eventually purchased K & W Glass Works.

There is a plain top version of an early K & W Glass Works box without the Feather Tree graphic. For Shiny Brites sourced from Corning Glass Works, the 1939 Feather Tree box is considered the first box.

1939 Feather Tree Box

There are at least four text versions of the original 1939 Feather Tree box. Sometimes a single factory is listed or a reference to Max Eckardt being the sole distributor.

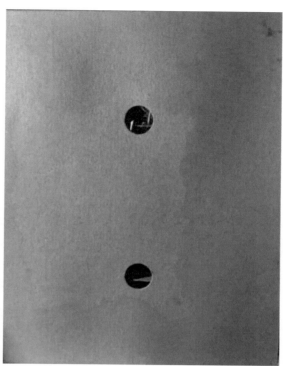

The Feather Tree box was also printed using blue ink. Typically missing from Feather Tree boxes are the top and bottom protective cardboard sleeves.

When packaging materials were needed to support the war effort, Shiny Brites were shipped in a rarely seen war stamp box.

After World War II, for their second box, Shiny Brites capitalized on patriotism by pairing Uncle Sam and Santa Claus. With the assistance of the Henry Ford Museum, the green Uncle Sam and Santa box is dated to 1946 and used well into the 1950s.

Common assortments included two bulbs of six colors: purple, silver, blue, red, green, and gold.

The red color scheme was issued after the green box possibly in 1949.

RETAIL TREE-1955

A shift to more in-store purchases created a need for a price holder. Often left blank, merchants were used to placing price stickers on the sides of boxes.

Retail Tree used festive bulbs on the left and right sides of the tree. Later, a new box die was made, replacing the tree with a see-through window. Retail Tree was printed in either a red or green version. Some original assortments sold four bulbs of three-stripes designs.

MERRY CHRISTMAS-HAPPY NEW YEAR-1955

The first two color box. Bulbs hanging from branches on the left and right hand sides of the tree are reminiscent of the Feather Tree box. The red box version of Merry Christmas-Happy New Year removed Uncle Sam and Santa.

CHRISTMAS TREE WINDOW BOX-1957

The iconic box Christmas Tree Window Box was the first to use the patented Alford carton, designed for shipping fruit. The box solidified Shiny Brite as a mass merchandiser and the leading brand of Christmas ornaments.

FESTIVE BRANCH

FESTIVE BULBS

Festive Branch-1964 The original Shiny Brite logo was modified. Note the snowflakes on the left and right sides which are repurposed in later years for discount store packaging.

Festive Bulbs-1963 Repurposed the bulbs from the 1955 Retail Tree graphic.

MODERN ERA

Holly Berries-1968

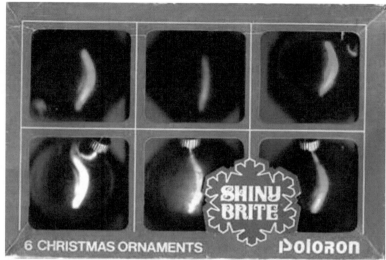

Mod Blue-1968

Red Medallion 1965 start of a Shiny Brite Product

Gold Scroll 1967 when the company was owned by Eckmar who revised the Shiny Brite Logo.

DECORATOR
GEORGE FRANKE SONS COMPANY

George Franke Sons Company in Baltimore, Maryland was the second-largest decorator of Corning Glass bulbs. Founded by George Franke, a German immigrant in 1868 the firm prospered as a box manufacturer. As the Christmas holiday became more popular, the Frankes added tinsel making and sold ornaments imported from Germany.

The firm, later led by son Edward Philip Franke as president, scrambled to keep the business going during World War I. During WW II, George Franke Sons Company was instrumental in producing tinsel dropped in the sky to scramble the radar of enemy aircraft.

After the war, prosperity returned and Philip Franke moved bulb decorating to a larger factory on Saratoga Street in Baltimore. Overshadowed by Max Eckardt's Shiny Brites, the Franke family controlled 25 percent of the American-made glass Christmas ornament market selling to retailers like Woolworth's and advertising in Life Magazine. After 100 years as a family firm, the company was sold in 1968

George Franke used the Red Bulb box in the 1940s and 1950s.

First Version George Franke Sons Box. Later version was two colors, red and green.

George Franke 1950s Snowflake Window Box. Note the use of cross branding with Life Magazine

EARLY YEARS

Blue Transparent   Purple Transparent

George Franke female employees handpainted bulbs.

POST-WAR

For a time after the war, George Franke Sons continued inserting tinsel into ornaments. Years of contact with its metal cap, electrolysis may have formed. Discoloration on the top of the Long Branch Tinsel may indicate vintage versus a modern replacement.

George Franke ornaments were blown by Corning Glass, and sold with a Made in USA cap with scalloped edges.

BEEHIVE WITH LONG BRANCH TINSEL

George Franke Sons always referred to this shape as a beehive never a spinning top.

POST-WAR SCENIC DESIGNS

While George Franke Sons did sell bells, decorated tops, ovals, and reflectors, and their version of the mushroom called a spiral shape, they specialized in screen printed designs.

Candle Centerpiece

Angel Musicians

Candy Cane

Toy Scene

Santa Chimney

Reindeer Wreath

Angel Choir

Candy Cane Bow

Santa with Reindeer

Reindeer Mates

Christmas Train

Merry Christmas With Tree

Santa with Sleigh

Choo Choo Express

Hand-Painted George Franke bulb

Poinsettia

Petals

Holly Spray

69

Angel Accord   Skating Scene   Whimsy

Holy Pilgrimage   Forest Scene   Village Scene

Joyous Noel

Font Merry Christmas

Merry Christmas Oval

Merry Christmas Candles

Merry Christmas Street Lamp

Seasons Greetings

One of the most popular of George
Franke's designs it was included in
single color sets and in assortments.
Blue was the most popular color of
1950s ornaments

Merry Christmas Old English

Seasons Cheer

Old Noel

O Come All Ye Faithful

Night Before Christmas

Hark the Herald

Shiny Brites and George Franke Sons raced to issue new decorations since both firms were selling the identical Corning bulb. If Shiny Brites issued a Jingle Bell lyric, the Frankes answered with an O Come All Ye Faithful bulb.

SPARKLE

To modernize the product line, by the mid-1960s, George Franke sold assortments of bulbs decorated with glitter and mica.

Round with Glitter Band

Glitter Top

Striped with Glitter

Decorated Top

George Franke never referred to this shape as a mushroom.

Bell with Mica

WOOLWORTH'S PACKAGING

Woolworth's created the demand for Christmas ornaments by importing German goods beginning in the 1880s. With domestic production secured through Corning Glass Works, Max Eckardt's Shiny Brites were the first American-made bulbs to be sold by the leading chain store.

Rare Woolworth's box used to sell imported European ornaments also printed in a blue version.

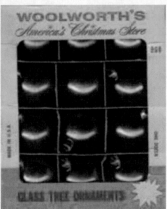

George Franke

In 1948, Woolworth's changed their supplier of glass ornaments to Santa Novelties owned by Harry Heim. When Heim's business folded, Shiny Brites resumed supplying the stores. After Max Eckardt sold his firm, George Franke Sons provided their decorated bulbs to Woolworth's. In 1965, Shiny Brites replaced George Franke. Since Woolworth's promoted their brand, consumers didn't know what firm was actually decorating their bulbs.

74

DISCOUNTER PACKAGING

Thrifty, Skaggs, Walgreens, Shopko, W.T. Grant, and Woolworth's wanted to sell more ornaments but struggled with the escalating price for one dozen. Package quantities were reduced to six, five, and three bulbs.

George Franke Christmas Trees

Shiny Brite Red Center Bow

Half Dozen packages sold in discount stores were introduced in the late 1950s.

White Church brought Santa Claus back to Shiny Brite boxes.

Festival Tree

The festival bulb and bulbs hanging on branches from the Christmas tree box were combined to sell jumbo six packs Old stock no longer desired by department stores was discounted and sold to drug stores, dime stores, and other retailers explaining the popularity of Uncle Sam and Santa through the 1950s, and the Christmas Tree Window box deep into the 1960s.

 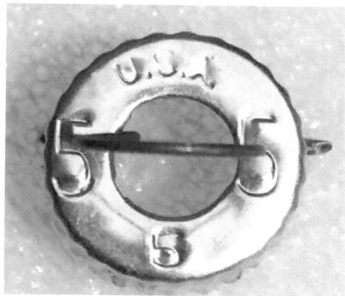

Drug stores, dime stores and discount stores sold feather tree ornaments and single ornaments priced at 5, 10, and 15 cents

George Franke Sons Company developed this impractical but delightful five pack box

Discount stores always sold 1" ornaments usually for a quarter. Shiny Brite Garland Window

By 1968 two tray packs of five ornaments were bundled together lowering the price as consumers drifted toward unbreakable and other styles of ornaments.

DISCOUNTER PACKAGING

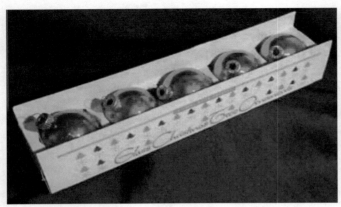

A popular trade dress for Shiny Brites in 1963 was Snowflakes and Trees. Packages of three, five, six, and a bundled twelve ornaments were offered.

Identical graphics were used to sell West German ornaments.

German caps have four crimped segments 1/8" in height with two equal sized prongs, the spring loop is 10/16" in length

78

CHRISTMAS TREE ORNAMENTS

Post-war West Germany ornaments used both metal caps and plastic. Max's son Harold imported ornaments under the Lanissa brand a composite of his daughters' names. L- for daughter Lynne-AN for Anne-ISSA for Alison who went by Lissa.

TREE TOPPERS

Tree toppers are impressive super-sized glass ornaments. Early 20th-century tree toppers were sold as part of an assortment. As Christmas trees grew taller, evolving from tabletop and feather varieties, there was increased demand in the 1930s for larger ornaments.

Many tree toppers were made in Europe, especially post-war when Max Eckardt re-established ornament manufacturing in West Germany.

Glass tree toppers fell out of favor when angels and electrified stars became popular Christmas tree decorations.

George Franke toppers were typically a single color and less ornate than those from West Germany. The Frankes marketed their product as Tree Top Ornaments selling both German and American made tree toppers. There are other instances when tree toppers were called tree top spires.

Note the discoloration at the end or what is called the pike you can see the residue from where the blown air was inserted to expand the molten glass to create the topper shape.

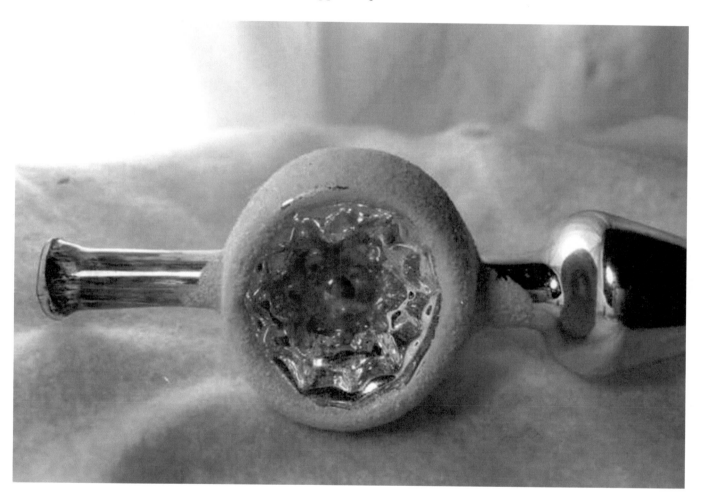

Shiny Brite Tree Topper

GLOBAL IDENTIFICATION

Pre-World War II, many ornaments were manufactured in Poland, Austria, Japan, and Czechoslovakia.

As the 1960s came to end, global sourcing became the norm for Christmas ornaments. Gingerbread people made in Japan, non-breakables bulbs that children could hang without fear, satin balls, and plastic 3D novelty shapes took hold ushering a modern feel to Christmas decorations.

Japan focused on the miniature market, 1½" or smaller.

Japan Merry Christmas

Austria caps are smooth edge with a 1 ¾" straight spring loop.

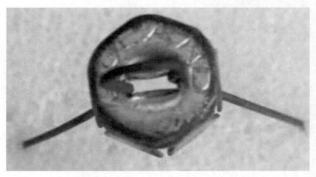

Many Poland caps have six crimped segments on the ¼" cap with two equal sized prongs. The spring loop is $1^{1/8}$" in length.

Pear-shaped bulbs with a tip are very common

Pre war ornament made in Poland

AMERICAN-MADE GLASS TREE ORNAMENTS

Inventor George Coby founded many businesses including Coby Glass in 1952. Initially, the company sourced Corning bulbs until George constructed a duplicate glass blowing machine in Rhode Island. By 1969, after numerous ownership changes of Shiny Brites and the sale of George Franke Sons, Coby Glass was the leading seller of American-made glass Christmas ornaments. By the 1970s, Coby created bulb blanks decorated and sold with images of Norman Rockwell, Looney Tunes, and popular scenes from Currier and Ives prints. Selling mostly rounds, Coby also manufactured a distinctive snowman shape.

PARAGON GLASS WORKS

In 1955, after Premier Glass was acquired by Shiny Brites, Angelo Paione relocated his new company Paragon Glass Works from New Jersey to Lewiston, Maine. The firm decorated bulbs and eventually resumed manufacturing miniature bulbs for automobiles.

Angelo Paione in his Paragon Glass Works factory

SANTA NOVELTIES

Harry Heim and his son Junior decorated Christmas windows in Baltimore, Maryland. Sensing opportunity, they hired glass blowers to craft ornaments from tubing. Heim pieced together equipment to decorate glass ornaments that he purchased from Corning Glass Works. Heim called his firm, Santa Novelties. With the help of financing from Woolworth's, Heim opened a second factory in San Diego, California to decorate bulbs.

Harry's true passion and his undoing was Santa Heim, a Christmas town for tourists. Financial miscues caused him to lose the town, the Woolworth's ornament business, and his factories. At auction, George Franke Sons acquired Heim's equipment for use in their Baltimore, Maryland facility.

Miro Star

Mirostar began as a manufacturer of mirrored reflectors, sold as an accessory to Christmas lights. Absorbed by Consolidated Novelties, a manufacturer of artificial Christmas trees, bulbs were added to their product line, a natural extension of selling trees.

The firm had a short tenure in glass bulbs, a few years during the 1960s, decorating Corning Glass bulbs. Sourcing only single colors, the ornament caps are similar to those used by George Franke Sons.

A major customer of Mirostar-Consolidated Novelties, was the W. T. Grant chain purchasing three pack jumbo ornaments.

Delta was the importing segment of Consolidated Novelties.

CARAMOOR PRODUCTS AND JOLLY HOLLY

The Shiny Brite story came full circle with Harold Eckardt. His father Max began his career as an importer before selling American made bulbs. Harold worked for the firm for decades before retiring and jumping back into the business. Harold and his wife June traveled the world and sourced ornaments for importation from Cali, Columbia. Like years of German produced ornaments and the work by hand painters during the war years, Jolly Holly and Caramoor Product ornaments some were hand painted.

Made in Columbia, South America

With the sudden death of Harold, Caramoor Products and the importation of glass ornaments from Columbia ended. The firm's duration was about eight years.

RAUCH INDUSTRIES

Marshall Rauch owned a successful textile factory in Gastonia, North Carolina. In 1962, at the request of a Spiegel Company, the firm perfected winding rayon thread around Styrofoam balls for Christmas ornaments. Rauch Industries expanded into producing and decorating glass bulbs.

Marshall was proud of his Jewish faith. Like many Christmas firms in the 1960s, he had a presence at the International Toy Center Building in New York City where other Christmas vendors knew him as a friend. Marshall led the firm until it was sold in 1995 to Syratech. Rauch became a market leader in the sale of Christmas decorations selling ornaments, snow, icicles, and garland. While breaking one of every four blown, Rauch often sold 200 million bulbs a year in the 2000s.

Lasting through multiple ownership changes, eventually Rauch Industries purchased the Christopher Radko brand and continues today selling to retailers.

Rauch caps are similar style to modern Premiers

ACKNOWLEDGEMENTS

Without my husband Karl, a talented video guy, my YouTube channel wouldn't exist. Without the channel, there wouldn't have been thousands of viewers who encouraged me to finally finish this project. Today is, tomorrow is not.

This is the third occasion I've gone to my graphic designer Alex Zezza with the fuzzy ask, "Can you make it pretty"? He never fails to dazzle me.

Thanks to Anne Demas, Angie Barnett, Edward Paione, and Jeff Kirks for sharing their photographs and images. My great resource for confirming ornament facts is Craig McManus who cares more about vintage Christmas than Santa Claus. I have never forgotten the kindness of Linda High, a fellow Golden Glow member, for helping launch what appears to be my new vocation of ornament teaching.

I continue to remember the staff at the Rakow Research Library in Corning, New York for their assistance with Immigrants, Ornaments, and Legacies, my first book, which made this one possible. All sources used in my work are documented in 358 end notes in the Immigrants book.

Life is about the people we meet and I've been blessed to be trusted by the Franke, Eckardt, and Paione families. I am also grateful to the countless employees of ornament manufacturers who went to work every day so that people could celebrate Christmas with colorful ornaments.

Index

Notes

Notes

Notes

Notes

Made in United States
Troutdale, OR
12/30/2024